Plus

Animal Offspring

Tigers and Their Cubs

Revised Edition

Margaret Hall

raintree

a Capstone company — publishers for children

Raintree is an imprint of Capstone Global Library Limited, a company incorporated in England and Wales having its registered office at 264 Banbury Road, Oxford, OX2 7DY – Registered company number: 6695582

www.raintree.co.uk
myorders@raintree.co.uk

ISBN 978 1 4747 5630 3 (hardback)
22 21 20 19 18
10 9 8 7 6 5 4 3 2 1

ISBN 978 1 4747 5640 2 (paperback)
23 22 21 20 19
10 9 8 7 6 5 4 3 2 1

British Library Cataloging in Publication Data
A full catalogue record for this book is available from the British Library.

Editorial Credits
Gina Kammer, editor; Sarah Bennett, designer; Morgan Walters, media researcher; Katy LaVigne, production specialist

Printed and bound in India

Acknowledgements
We would like to thank the following for permission to reproduce photographs:
Getty Images: CHARLY TRIBALLEAU, 9; Shutterstock: Africa Studio, 13, Anan Kaewkhammul, 11, left 20, chanyut Sribua-rawd, right 20, Cynthia Kidwell, Cover, Dennis Jacobsen, 5, George Lamson, 15, Julian W, 17, neelsky, right 21, otsphoto, left 21, Raj Wildberry, 1, Volodymyr Burdiak, 19, Xseon, 7

Every effort has been made to contact copyright holders of material reproduced in this book. Any omissions will be rectified in subsequent printings if notice is given to the publisher.

Contents

Tigers

Tigers are mammals.

Tigers are large cats
with whiskers.

A female is a tigress.

Young tigers are cubs.

A male tiger mates
with a tigress.
The male tiger leaves
before the cubs are born.

Tiger cubs

A tigress gives birth to two

or three cubs.

The cubs drink milk

from her body.

Cubs are born blind and deaf.

They can see and

hear after two weeks.

Growing up

Cubs rest during the day.

They grow quickly.

13

The tigress licks the cubs

to clean them.

She keeps them safe.

The tigress teaches the cubs
to hunt and find food.

Cubs live with their mothers

for about two years.

Then each cub leaves

to find its own home.

Watch tigers grow

birth

adult after
about four years

Glossary

birth to be born; a tigress gives birth to a group of cubs

blind unable to see; tiger cubs are born with their eyes closed; their eyes open after two weeks

deaf unable to hear; cubs can hear after two weeks

mammal warm-blooded animal that has a backbone and hair or fur; female mammals feed milk to their young

mate join together to produce young

tigress adult female tiger

whisker one of the long, stiff hairs near the mouth of an animal

Plus

Animal Offspring

Tigers and Their Cubs

Revised Edition

Margaret Hall

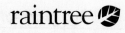

raintree

a Capstone company — publishers for children

Raintree is an imprint of Capstone Global Library Limited, a company incorporated in England and Wales having its registered office at 264 Banbury Road, Oxford, OX2 7DY – Registered company number: 6695582

www.raintree.co.uk
myorders@raintree.co.uk

ISBN 978 1 4747 5630 3 (hardback)
22 21 20 19 18
10 9 8 7 6 5 4 3 2 1

ISBN 978 1 4747 5640 2 (paperback)
23 22 21 20 19
10 9 8 7 6 5 4 3 2 1

British Library Cataloging in Publication Data
A full catalogue record for this book is available from the British Library.

Editorial Credits
Gina Kammer, editor; Sarah Bennett, designer; Morgan Walters, media researcher; Katy LaVigne, production specialist

Printed and bound in India

Acknowledgements
We would like to thank the following for permission to reproduce photographs:
Getty Images: CHARLY TRIBALLEAU, 9; Shutterstock: Africa Studio, 13, Anan Kaewkhammul, 11, left 20, chanyut Sribua-rawd, right 20, Cynthia Kidwell, Cover, Dennis Jacobsen, 5, George Lamson, 15, Julian W, 17, neelsky, right 21, otsphoto, left 21, Raj Wildberry, 1, Volodymyr Burdiak, 19, Xseon, 7

Contents

Tigers

Tigers are mammals.

Tigers are large cats

with whiskers.

A female is a tigress.

Young tigers are cubs.

A male tiger mates
with a tigress.
The male tiger leaves
before the cubs are born.

Tiger cubs

A tigress gives birth to two
or three cubs.
The cubs drink milk
from her body.